The Consumer's Guide to Closet Design

by
Denise Butchko, RSD

Registered Storage Designer

Award Winning Closet Designer

*Helping People Design More Effective Space
For Better Living*

Dedication: If you love beautiful, organized spaces, then this book is dedicated to YOU! It's about making the world a more beautiful place one closet at a time.

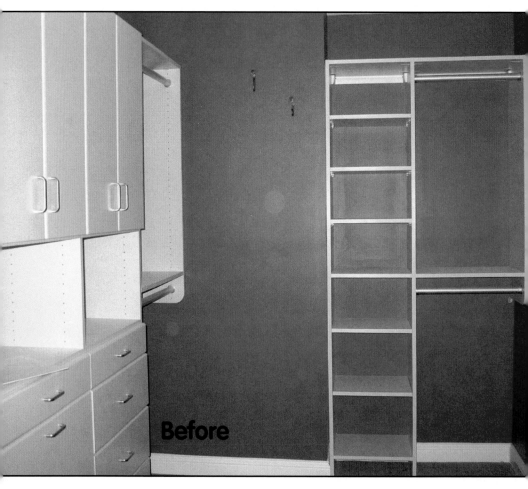

Before

Closet Before

This white melamine closet was replaced with the beautiful stained mahogany wood. I revamped the design for a much more effective use of space and stellar aesthetic.

We used leather for the countertop and drawer and door pulls. The upper doors are frosted glass, aluminum framed doors.

If you'd like to see the plans and more details, check them out on my You Tube Channel (Denise Butchko) under "Closet Design Reviews". And while you're there checking things out, I'd love to have you subscribe to my channel.

After

Closet After

Denise Butchko

Award Winning Closet Designer
Judge for Closet Industry Top Shelf Design Awards
Digital Correspondent/Blogger for Woodworking Network
Association of Closet and Storage Professionals
National Kitchen & Bath Association

ButchkoAndCompany.com

Before

After

Before

After

This "Stairway To Heaven" closet is Oak stained to match the rest of the millwork in the house. The puzzling design and engineering feat is still a personal favorite.

Contents

Introduction:

It's a rare person (I've yet to meet one) who doesn't appreciate the benefits of having a Walk In Closet.

Being able to easily see and access all of your clothing and accessories is one of the best time saving, life-organizing tools EVER.

Yet, if it's not designed well, you can actually end up wasting space. And wasting space in one of the most high demand spaces in the home is a costly mistake that impacts life on a daily basis.

Closet space is high on function. In fact, the demand for space to function well in closets is even higher than in kitchens.

Think about it.

You probably have 24" deep base cabinets in your kitchen with a shelf or two inside the cabinets.

You then put things like pots and pans or serving dishes inside these cabinets. Or you have boxes of things like cereal, crackers and pasta that get stored inside these cabinets.

You can stack these items and they don't easily fall over because they are not "soft". They retain their shape (unlike sweaters).

Yet clothing is "soft". Some of it is on hangers and some items are folded. Others are good for baskets (like socks or gym clothes, pajamas or dirty laundry) and some fare better on shelves.

So how do you achieve maximized storage with a beautiful aesthetic?

Read on to gain insights.

How To Design a Reach In Closet

- Reach-In closets generally are wall-to-wall unless there is an obstacle. Wall-to-wall requires a "hard" measurement. Once the hard measurement is determined, subtract ¼" to ½" to allow for flexibility in your design.

- Keep in mind that the fewer sections you divide the closet into will make items more accessible and lower the price.

- Some guidelines for how many sections to divide the closet into based upon the width of the closet:

3 feet	1 – 2 sections
4 feet	2 sections
5 feet	2 – 3 sections
6 feet	3 sections
7 feet	3 – 4 sections
8 feet	3 – 4 sections
9 feet	4 sections
10 feet	4 – 5 sections

- Your key measurement for a Reach-In is taken across the back wall. Do not take this measuremens in front of the clothing; always take it on the back wall.

- Measure the depth of both side walls. It's very important to remember that 24" or more is required to hang clothes. If the closet is less than 22" deep, hanging should be avoided.

- Standard height is 84" from the floor. Anything higher is difficult to access because of the front header.

- Measure the return walls, ceiling, baseboard heights and any obstacles.

- If drawers or baskets are to be included, they need to be considered first and located so that they can be fully opened. This may create a very small (16 to 18" wide) section between the side wall and the drawers, which is hard to access unless there are no return walls.

- Place hanging sections in the hard to reach areas like deep returns OR in the middle section of a long closet that has two openings with doors.

- When placing hanging in the middle space, try to go beyond the span of the front wall area so panels don't block access. If the front wall between the doors is 20," make that middle hanging section at least 36" wide.

- If there is an access panel or other obstacle on the back wall, design a hanging section in front of the panel that still allows access (so the section spans the width of the access panel).

- The deeper the panels, the harder it is to reach items because there's less open space in front of the installed structure.

- Most top shelves in Reach-In closets are used to accommodate larger, soft items such as pillows and blankets. The reason for this is once you install a system that's 14" deep, you're only left with 10" of open "front" space to fit things up and onto the top shelf.

How To Design a Walk In Closet

The First Steps:

Here are the parameters I use and steps I follow to professionally measure and design Walk In Closet space:

Measuring:

Measuring is key for obvious reasons. Cabinetry and panels need to fit in to the space and items need to be accessible. Drawers need to close and doors need to open.

I recommend starting in this order:

1. Back wall measurements
2. Left side wall measurements
3. Right side wall measurement
4. Left front return wall
5. Right front return wall
6. Ceiling heights(s)
7. Baseboard height and depth
8. Door Height and width
9. Any outlet locations
10. Any light switch locations
11. Any other obstacles like steam mechanicals, access panels and vents

Remember that the tape measure should be held tight to the wall. Ideally you should measure at three different heights and use the smallest measurement. Even in new construction, it's rare to find walls that are perfectly square.

If you have a good quality laser tape measure, use that. Measure at least three times – a low point on the wall – a mid point on the wall – and a high point on the wall.

Use the smallest number of the three and subtract 1/4" to 1/2" inch from that number. You should subtract 1/4" if the wall measures less than eight feel in width and 1/2" if the wall is longer than eight feet. This allows for uneven walls, easier installation and easier adjustability. It's better to have small gaps on the side walls than to have things be too big or too tight.

Too big means lots of work and money in recutting things and too tight makes the closet system difficult to adjust as you use it.

After you have all of that information written down and drawn out on "grid" paper, you can begin planning the structural elements of your closet system. As you start to do this, here are some things to pay attention to:

Things To Pay Attention To

1. Decide your top priorities. Is the top goal to fit as much stuff into the space as possible so you use every inch? Then function rules. If you also want beauty and function, then aesthetics must balance with storage function. There are always trade-offs.

2. If the closet is wider than it is long (as you stand in the doorway looking in) I recommend starting the design process by putting hanging on the short walls (ideally double hang). Then determine drawer locations (usually centered on the back wall in line with the entrance because drawers look the nicest). Build the long hang, medium hang, half and half and shelving from there.

3. Shelving that's 14" deep is good by entrances because it's often used for shoes, which are put on last and taken off first, as you enter and exit the closet. I actually prefer 12" deep shelving if you're using it for shoes and 16" deep shelving for storing folded items.

The 14" depth became an industry standard when California Closets was trying to simplify manufacturing and installation. I've never loved it, particularly since 14" deep drawers for clothing is super shallow.

Wall-to-Wall systems (with hard measurements) require a tight fit. "Short" walls are frequently used for Double Hang. So as you are looking at the dimensions in your plan view, try designing the space with Double Hang on those short walls. Double Hang also provides the biggest ROI because it literally doubles your hanging capacity from what likely existed before (a rod and a shelf).

4. Be sure not to put drawers behind a door that opens into the closet.

5. Avoid Double Hang as the first section as you enter because it feels like a wall of clothing coming at you, which is another reason why it works well on the back wall.

6. If you've designed Double Hang on the short walls, the next sections on the adjacent walls should be anything BUT Double Hang (unless you're allowing at least 30" of space from the back wall to the start of the new section). While the DH (Double Hang) configuration is one that's used in almost every closet, it also feels like a wall of clothing due to having two levels of hanging with shoulder garments.

7. Corners are important to deal with in a Walk-In Closet. While more complex solutions exist, the majority of the time you can incorporate one that's very easy. Simply allow 24" (minimum) to 30" from the back wall before starting the section on the adjacent wall. This allows for the depth of the clothing plus a couple of inches for reaching in to get them.

This measurement (the 24-30") is one that can be adjusted up or down based upon the space you have to work with and is referred to as a "soft" measurement. What happens in this space is a "bridge shelf" is installed, which spans the width of the space. This allows for a continuous storage shelf around the perimeter.

8. Be particularly attentive to the "short" walls in the closet, as it is likely these will be "hard" measurements, with the design going wall-to-wall (versus having a "bridge" shelf that allows for the top piece to be cut-to-fit on site).

9. If the depth of the front return walls is at least 24" deep (which then also means that the closet is at least 72" wide), hanging can be accommodated/designed into both of the adjacent walls. If you have less than 24" between the sidewall and the entrance, you need to use shelving and drawers/baskets or else the hanging will interfere with the doorway clearances. Translated, this means that you will literally walk right in to the garments as you enter the closet.

10. You need a minimum of 24" for a walkway in a closet (between the two sides or around an island or peninsula). This is narrower than ADA standards, so if the client has special needs, this dimension needs to be wider. And keep in mind that this is a closet so the smaller pathway is tolerated in trade-off of maximizing space.

Hanging Systems vs. Floor-Based Systems

Hanging Systems:

- Installed by using a metal hanging strip (suspension rail) that is anchored into studs. Panels are attached to and supported by suspension rail.

- Suspension rail is visible.

- No panels go to the floor.

- More utilitarian approach than Floor Based Systems.

- Easier to install.

- Allows more flexibility in your measurements. You don't have to be as accurate.

- Limits your future adjustability options.

- Not advisable to install in front of a pocket door.

- Depth of these systems should not exceed 18". Anything deeper than 16" should really be Floor-Based.

These basic
Reach In Closets
demonstrate the
elements of:

- short panels

- wall hanging strips

- continuous line boring.

Floor-Based System:

Vertical Panels rest on the floor and are attached to the walls.

- Allows for easy changes to the system in the future because the basic structure is in place. Hanging, shelves and drawers can be easily added/subtracted.

- Baseboards on side walls will be cut away. The Vertical Panels will need to be installed flush to the return walls.

- Does not typically require a hanging strip across back wall. Takes longer to install. Requires more material required. Measurements have to be more accurate.

The Placement of Things - Deciding What To Put Where

If the closet measures 48" wide or less on the longest wall:

You can only do an "L" shaped design. Hanging should go on the back (short) wall. Use the sidewall with the deepest return for shelves/ drawers/baskets. The other long wall can have hooks.

If the closet measures 54" – 60" on the longest wall:

Hanging should still go on the back wall and possibly one sidewall (with the deepest return). Only 12" deep shelving on the opposite wall allows for a 24" clearance (minimum).

Anything under 72"

cannot accommodate hanging on both, opposing walls. This is common.
Builders, developers and architects still don't consider actual storage
capacity when they decide on the size of the closet. It looks large
when it's empty, but oftentimes the location of the door, the size of the
return walls and the width really net no more storage than a Reach-In
configuration.

If the closet measures 72" – 84" in width –

Hanging should still go on the back wall. Both sidewalls can be used
for hanging, though this configuration provides for only the minimum
clearance of a 24" walkway. Designing hanging on only one of the
sidewalls (with the deepest return) and shelves/drawers/baskets on the
other sidewall is optimal.

If you have over 84" in width –

Allows for the most options and configuration choices. Aesthetics can be
played with when you have this much space.

120"

is required as the minimum width to include a one-sided or narrow
island or peninsula. That means doors or drawers that open on just one
side (versus both sides).

144"

allows for a two-sided island or peninsula

The "Lingo" - Closet Industry Terms

Most closet systems are based on the 32 millimeter system. That means there's a hole drilled approximately every 1 1/4". This allows for adjustability.

Double Hang – upper and lower short hanging in one section; two rods. Shortest items should be hung on the top rod so they don't overshadwo the items on the lower rod. Items with big shoulders are better on the lower rod. However, if you're petite and have a taller partner, you can share the space according to height.

Medium Hang – rod with 2-3 shelves above, used mostly for hanging pants long (versus folded in half over a hanger). For petite people, serves as Long Hang. This is most typically used for hanging pants by the top or the cuff (versus folding them in half over a hanger).

Long Hang – rod with 1-2 shelves above, used mostly for hanging dresses.

Half and Half – lower section of short hang, upper section of shelving. This is one of the best, most useful configurations because both hanging as well as items on shelves are easy to see and reach.

Rods – typically installed approximately 11" from the back wall. Can be round or oval. Thickness of rods determines length it can span without risk of bending.

System Height —Indicates the vertical measurement from the floor to the top shelf of the closet system. Predominantly 84" and 96", but can be any number.

Inside Dimension – the actual width of the section between the upright panels.

Outside Dimension – the width of the section that includes the upright panels.

Hard Measurements – precise measurements that go wall-to-wall and will have sections that completely fill the wall space.

Soft Measurements – These wall measurements typically have Bridge Shelves that connect adjacent sections for continuous top shelf storage. Because the Bridge shelf is easy to cut on site, or cut down if it's too big, we refer to these wall measurements as "soft" because there's a little bit of flexibility. We also refer to measurements as "soft" when the closet sections don't fill the entire space or go wall-to-wall.

Bridge Shelf – the top shelf connector piece that is typically between 10" and 14" wide. Designing with a bridge shelf allows for one continuous storage shelf along the top of the system. These can often be cut-to-fit in the field. Most DIY closets don't have bridge shelves.

Panel – the vertical pieces of material that divide the sections, typically 84" and 96" in Floor Based Systems and 48" and 60" in Hanging Systems.

Wall Hanging Systems/Floor Based Systems/Cabinetry and Millwork – Hanging systems have short panels that do not go all the way to the floor. Floor Based systems have vertical panels that go all the way to the floor. They typically include a toe-kick. In traditional closet systems, the vertical panel is shared. In cabinets/millwork each section is its' own "box" (cabinet).

Standard Placements:

Standard Rod Placements (height to top of rod from floor):

Double Hang: 40 ½" and 82"

Medium Hang: 54"

Long Hang: 66"

Standard Placement Heights for Accessories:

Valet Rail/Pole: 70" from floor unless otherwise specified

                60" from floor for children

Belt Rack: 50" or the length of the belt + 2"

                42" for children

                Install in LH, on wall or outside of side panel

Tie Racks: 78" and 40" for two racks, one above the other

                72" for a single tie rack

                Install on wall or outside of side panel

Iron & Board
Holder: 60" from floor or per customer preference

Mop & Broom
Holder: 54" from floor

Average Dimensions of Typical Clothing Items:

Hanging:

Garment		Width	Length including hanger
Skirts	DH	1-2"	30-44"
Dresses	M-LH	1-2"	44-66"
Blouses	DH	½"-1 ½"	28-36"
Women's Suits/Jackets	DH	2-4"	30-42"
Men's Suits/Jackets	DH	2-4"	38-44"
Men's Shirts	DH	1-3"	38-40"
Adult Coats	M-LH	4-7"	44-66"
Outerwear Jackets	M	4-7"	40-48"
Pants, hanging long	D-MH	1-2"	41-52"
Pants, hanging folded	DH	1-2"	28-32"
Robes	M-LH	2-4"	44-66"
Women's Formal Dresses	XLH	3-8"	70-78"

Folding:

Garment	Width	Depth
Sweaters, Jeans	10-14"	14-16"
T-shirts	10-12"	12-14"
Towels/Sheets	14-16"	14-16"
Blankets	18-24"	14-18"
Shoes – Women's	Average pair is 7-8" wide	
Shoes – Men's	Average pair is 9" wide	

Do It Yourself or Hire a Pro

Good closet designers are very passionate about what they do. They're part designer, part therapist, part engineer and part puzzle solver. Designing closet space effectively requires a left brain/right brain balance that most people don't quickly shift back and forth between.

So I encourage you to invest in the expertise of someone with experience. Couples therapy is expensive and there are many who think that this "simple" project will be a no brainer, only to have controversy on the home front.

And good custom closet designers are different in many ways from "a man with a van and plan". You might get a closet system installed, but it's functionality may be limited once you actually start using. Or it may not truly maximize the space or provide you with the best options. What looks effortless requires tremendous brain power.

Yes, there are many closet companies who come out "for free" and do a "consultation". But as this young, progressive industry gets its' sea legs, you'll see the professionals stepping away from free sales scenarios and requiring a financial commitment much the same as architects, interior designers and kitchen and bath designers. That's because as we evolve, complexities and options increase. We're going beyond "plug and play" and into custom design. The professional trade organization for this industry is the Association of Closet and Storage Professionals (http://closets.org).

Here are some insights on the role of a professional closet designer.

It's the Closet Designers job to provide custom storage solutions that accommodate the needs of the client, have structural integrity and maximize the effectiveness of that space within workable parameters (walls, obstacles, etc.)

It's also the Designers job to know what types of solutions work best for the different items that are typically stored in closets (for example, 12" deep shelves for shoes, 14-16" deep shelves for folded items).

Designers need to ask a lot of questions about how the client wants the space to function and what items will be stored in it.

In order to differentiate between a Closet Designer and a Professional Organizer (the most common comparison), the following information should be helpful:

Pros Who Prevent Closet Chaos

There are 5 different types of professionals that a person can hire to help them in their closets:

The Professional Organizer – it is this person's job to go through each and every item in your closet with you and first determine if you keep it or release it. Then they take what's left and literally organize it by categories or colors or any other number of systems. They typically incorporate existing storage solutions like boxes and bags and shelving, though they sometimes bring in closet designers to design/configure the space.

The Image Consultant – it is this person's job to lead you through discovering the best colors, shapes, styles and fabrics for you, your body type and your lifestyle, incorporating your goals, intentions and how you wish to be perceived. Highly, highly recommended. Check out the Association of Image Consultants International

The Stylist – it is this person's job to find the most current, stylish outfits for you to wear. If you work with an Image Consultant, you won't need a Stylist.

The Tailor/Seamstress – it is this person's job to make sure garments fit you perfectly. They often work in tandem with Image Consultants and Stylists.

The Closet Designer – it is this person's job to provide the structure for storage. They plan the space so it accommodates the needs of the client, has structural integrity and maximizes the effectiveness of that

space. They design custom storage solutions. They're trained in how to configure and build so you get as much as possible to work as effectively as possible in terms of storage. They can recommend simple melamine systems or more complex wood systems. They can be basic in design or elaborate, with added moldings and materials like glass, wood and metal. As the closet industry has evolved, so have the design solutions. You can now really get your "dream, boutique-like" closet if you're willing to allocate the resources to having it designed and built.

Beyond the Closet

There's much, much more to well designed closet and custom storage space than is covered in this small, introductory book. In fact, I teach an online course called Closet Design 101 (Closet Design Course 101) as well as consult with companies who want to add closets to their product lines and training to their sales staff.

I started on the path of closet design shortly after I moved from Indiana to Chicago. I worked with a large, local, company in the market. I then spent six years in a more custom shop learning to design with much broader parameters. And then ventured out on my own to create the solutions and service that met with my personal and professional standards. If you'd like to know more of my story, you can find it on Linked In (http://www.linkedin.com/denisebutchko) or on my website (http://www.butchkoandcompany.com/consumer/)

My perspective is as unique as yours:

Good design inspires me. It excites me. It prompts me in to action.

I'm also all about the beauty. And the privilege of creating beauty by collaborating with people on creating their "dream closet" is one of my favorite things to do.

Yet I balance that with the importance of function. Working on custom storage solutions throughout the home that help keep things organized is a great privilege. And I do that by working with interior designers and architects in the early planning stages to allocate the optimal space dimensions so we can design and build beautiful, functional solutions.

I bring an image consulting and Fashion Feng Shui background to my custom storage design. I learned engineering and manufacturing principles along the way.

And I bring a "we're all connected" and "all of our efforts combined can serve a great purpose".

One of my missions is to make the world a more beautiful space – one closet or home office at a time.

So teaching others to incorporate great design principles that contribute toward achieving that goal makes it feel even more attainable. As a Top Shelf Design Award winner, member of the Association of Closet and Storage Professionals, Registered Storage Designer, digital correspondent/blogger for The Woodworking Network, and judge of the Top Shelf Design Awards (closet industry design competition), I feel well positioned to do that.

I'd like to thank you for participating in the movement to take great design into the closet.

I hope I've opened your eyes to the value of well designed closet space.

What Do You Do Now?

So you've read some great info on how to approach the designing of closet space.

And now you're making the decision about whether to head on over to a home improvement store and buy your supplies or consult with a design professional to create your closet space.

While I don't speak on behalf of home improvement stores, I can speak to the professionalism of members of The Association of Closet and Storage Professionals (ACSP).

This professional association dedicated to home storage professionals is one that I am an active member of. I am also a member of the first class of Registered Storage Designers.

As a small association dedicated to creating professionalism in the field, we've created a certification program and are working to grow awareness.

So, should you decide to seek professional assistance with your project, I would encourage you to visit the website for the association and look for a practicing member in your area.

Here's a link to the site: http://www.closets.org.
It's a link to the Association of Closet and Storage Professionals.

And please take a moment to join me online by following me on these platforms. I appreciate the opportunity to get your thoughts on content that I create and share. And you'll get even more value (in addition to your purchasing the book) from continued connections where I share a variety of info and videos about the closets and design.

http://www.houzz.com/pro/denisebutchko/denise-butchko-butchkoand-company

 Http://www.YouTube.com/DeniseButchko

 Http://www.Twitter.com/DeniseButchko

 Http://www.Facebook.com/ButchkoAndCompany

 Http://www.Instagram.com/DeniseButchko

 Http://www.Pinterest.com/DeniseButchko

Made in the USA
Middletown, DE
24 February 2021